Contents

MP3457 Writing Well

Answers

Page 1:
Identifying Complete Sentences

1. NS
2. S period
3. S period
4. NS
5. NS
6. NS
7. S period
8. S ?
9. NS
10. S period

Page 2:
Constructing Sentences
Answers will vary.

Page 3:
Appositives

1. ,Hetty Sullivan,   2. ,my English teacher?
3. ,an old ship,   4. ,a sturdy oak,   5. ,a man of many talents,
6. Our new car, a Honda, uses very little gas.
7. We called Ms. Edwards, the art editor.
8. Terry, this is Chico, my brother.
9. Pat, the girl in the yellow sweater, likes outdoor life.
10. A young singer, Michael Jackson, captivated the whole country, or Michael Jackson, a young singer, captivated the whole country.

Page 4:
Clauses and Phrases

1. P
2. P
3. C
4. C
5. P
6. C
7. P
8. C
9. C
10. C
11. C
12. C

Page 5:
Expanding Sentences
Answers will vary.

Page 6:
Complex Sentences
Answers will vary, but might include the following:

1. The roads were closed because the snow fell heavily.
   Because the snow fell heavily, the roads were closed.
2. The leader made a fire before the campers set up their tents.
   Before the campers set up their tents, the leader made a fire.
3. Since the weather turned warm, Pam plays tennis every day.
   Pam plays tennis every day since the weather turned warm.
4. We will go skating if Paul will come with us.
   If Paul will come with us, we will go skating.
5. When Marty struck out, the game was over.
   The game was over when Marty struck out.

Teacher: The use of the comma with adverbial clauses: If a clause functions as an adverb, it answers when, where, why, or how.) Place a comma after an adverbial clause if it introduces a sentence.

Page 7:
Compound Sentences

2. Dr. Tibbs was visiting but wife welcomed
3. Mr Blewett was transferred so Mr. Ewell was sent
4. I was worried for he was
5. he was not interested nor did he care
6. stories appeal but stories appeal
7. , or S
8. , so S
9. predicate
10. , but S
11. , yet S
12. subject

Page 8:
Combining Sentences
Answers will vary. Possible answers:

1. Otters and beavers have two layers of fur.
2. A beaver uses its front teeth to cut down trees and to peel off bark.
3. Otters swim rapidly and dive for fish.
4. Beautiful, red cardinals ate the seed daily.
5. Melting snow can cause many disastrous floods.
6. Flood waters recede slowly.
7. Amy, my sister, goes to Pershing High School.
8. Ted, Tom's brother, walks with us once in awhile.
9. Mary lost her paper for English class.
10. Lisa watched a comedy because she felt like laughing.
11. We ate dessert after he opened the gifts.

Page 9:
Topic Sentences

1. too broad 2. too broad 3. satisfactory 4. too broad
5. satisfactory Note: you may wish to have the students write reasons for deciding which topics were too broad or give examples that would be satisfactory.

Page 10:
Writing Paragraphs

This page helps the class to notice what makes the difference between a good paragraph and a poor one. Does the paragraph have a definite topic sentence? Do all the other sentences relate to and help develop the topic? Is there a logical order to the sentences? After the students have read and graded the paragraphs, they should be ready to justify their evaluation in relation to the criteria already discussed. They should apply the same criteria to writing their own topic sentences and finally to writing their own well organized paragraphs. It may be useful to have the students read their topic sentences aloud to each other for criticism before they begin writing.

Answers: A: U   B: G   C: E

ii

Answers

Page 11:
Using Exact Words
Answers will vary.

Page 12:
Personification and Hyperbole
1. personification 2. personification 3. hyperbole
2. personification 5. hyperbole 6. personification
7. personification 8. hyperbole 9. personification 10. hyperbole

Page 13:
Metaphors and Similes
I. 1. metaphor 2. simile 3. simile 4. metaphor 5. metaphor
6. simile 7. simile 8. simile 9. simile 10. metaphor 11. metaphor
II. Answers will vary.

Page 14:
Descriptive Paragraph
Answers will vary.

Page 15:
Words Create Moods
  This page is most beneficial if handled as a class exercise, until students can develop moods on their own. The paragraphs might best be done as homework exercises, ready for the next class period. It is suggested that some paragraphs be read aloud to see if the desired mood was obtained. The last exercise should prove to be a good culminating activity that will test to see if the student has mastered moods in his writing. Have students bring in samples of cartoons or phrases in stories from the newspaper in which a specific mood has been created. Share some with the class.

1. happy mood: youngsters splashing in a lake; chirping birds and chattering squirrels; blue skies and brilliant sunlight; a warm fire; loud laughter; spectators cheering. What does each phrase have that would make the reader feel HAPPY, not SAD? The paragraph should produce a happy feeling. Let members of the class be the judge. Anxious mood: low rumble of thunder; bending, clutching trees; howling in the distance; swaying shadows; trembling hands; trees moaning in the wind; a muddy river. Paragraphs and stories will differ, but should meet the requirements of the assignment.

Page 16:
The Speaker's Mood
  This exercise deals with moods, but not in connection with the setting or atmosphere. This page deals with the way in which a speaker within a story sets a mood. This kind of mood projection gives insight into the person speaking so that the reader will have a better understanding of the speaker's personality and the situation he is in.
  Read over the list of words that will describe the mood of the speakers in the exercise on this page. Encourage the use of the dictionary for defining unfamiliar words. This could be a group exercise in familiarization.

More than one answer will apply, in several cases. Suggested answers are given, the first being the most acceptable. 1. envious, discontented, sad; 2. guilty, distressed; 3. disgusted, angry; 4. sympathetic; 5. vexed, distressed, disgusted; 6. triumphant, joyful; 7. mischievous

Page 17:
Direct Quotation

Dialogue

  Have the students read aloud the various words suggested that may be used instead of "said." Discuss the picture transmitted by the words. In doing this exercise, the students can gain additional practice in punctuating direct quotations.

  "Sandy, you are too little to use my camera. Put it down!" shouted Gene.
  "But I just wanted to see how it worked," begged Sandy.
  'All right. I'll show you how it works," answered Gene. "but then go away so I can work."

  Mary stated, "It is a lovely day for skating on Turner's Pond."
  "Yes, Mary, and there are some of our friends," remarked Jo, "over by the fire."
  Suddenly Mary shrieked, "Turn back! The ice is breaking!"

  "My throat is so sore," whispered Heather, "I don't know how I will be able to sing my solo."
  "Maybe they could cancel your part," Lee suggested.
  "Oh no! My grandmother has come from Albany to hear me sing," groaned Heather, "and she would be so disappointed."

Page 18 — 21:
Answers will vary.

Page 22:
5 Ws in Reporting
  (Answers will vary. The following are included only as guidelines). Jay Jacks: Who? Jay Jacks; What? received a plaque; When? Saturday; Where? at a dinner; Why? for saving two small children from drowning. (While the actual rescue may seem more important to your class, the article was written because of the plaque.)
  Ho Hum: Who? the Ho Hums; What? will give a benefit performance; When? February 14, 2002; Where? Hope Auditorium; Why? for Organ Fund research.
  Storm: Who? people of Faraway, Maine; What? suffering from severe blizzard; When? last night; Where? Faraway, Maine; Why? town was blanketed by 24-inch snowfall,

Answers

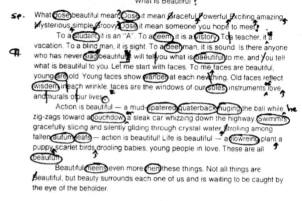

Identifying Complete Sentences

Write S if the words are a sentence and NS if not a sentence. Add end punctuation for each sentence.

S or NS   . ?

_____ 1. Around the neighborhood every evening after dinner   ____

_____ 2. The McIntoshes flew non-stop to London   ____

_____ 3. They went to visit friends in England   ____

_____ 4. Because in some of the places on the map   ____

_____ 5. All of the many interesting places in the travel book   ____

_____ 6. Leaving for Scotland and Ireland in the morning   ____

_____ 7. *Pippi Longstocking* was written by Astrid Lindgren   ____

_____ 8. Are you afraid to go into the house alone at midnight   ____

_____ 9. The friendly black dog down the street   ____

_____ 10. Traveling in the car, we thought the day seemed very long   ____

Every sentence contains a **subject** *and a* **predicate**. *A* **noun** *or* **pronoun** *is the main part of the subject. A* **verb** *is the main part of the predicate.*

On another paper or on the back of this sheet, write six sentences about your favorite holiday or season. After you have finished, cross out either the subject or predicate in three of the sentences to make them incomplete. Rewrite the three complete and three incomplete sentences below. Give your paper to a classmate. Ask your classmate to check the sentences that are complete.

_____

_____

_____

_____

_____

_____

_____

_____

_____

1

Constructing Sentences

Write words on the lines to make simple sentences. Use the parts of speech as indicated. You may add articles (a, an, the) to the nouns as needed.

Remember:

Nouns name persons, places, things. **Adjectives** describe nouns.
Verbs show action or state of being. **Adverbs** tell how, when, where.
Active verbs are *run, look, yell*. **Prepositions** connect a noun to a
Linking verbs are *is, am, are*. word before it.

Examples:

Dogs run.
noun   active verb

Big dogs run fast.
adj. noun   verb adj.

Quickly the ball flew over the fence.
adverb   noun act. prep.   noun
                 verb

The dog was brown.
   noun linking adj.
         verb

1. _____ _____ .
    noun   verb

2. _____ _____ _____ .
    noun   linking verb   adjective

3. _____ _____ _____ .
    noun   active verb   adverb

4. _____ _____ _____ _____ .
    noun   active verb preposition   noun

5. _____ _____ _____ _____ .
    noun   active verb adjective   noun (object)

6. _____ _____ _____ .
    adjective   noun   verb

7. _____ _____ _____ _____ .
    adverb   noun   active verb noun (object)

8. _____ _____ _____ _____ .
    adverb   adjective   noun   verb

9. _____ _____ _____ _____ _____
    adverb   adjective   noun   preposition noun

_____ _____ .
active verb noun (object)

10. _____ _____ _____ _____
    adjective   adjective   adjective   noun

_____ _____ .
verb   adverb

2

Appositives

An appositive is an expression (a word or group of words) that explains or identifies a noun or pronoun that comes just before it in a sentence. Appositives are set off from the rest of the sentence by commas.

Example: Arnie won the first prize, a trip to Hawaii.
(The appositive, **a trip to Hawaii**, describes the noun, **prize**.)

An appositive is an expression (word or group of words) that explains or identifies a noun or pronoun that comes just before it in a sentence.

Place commas where needed to separate each appositive from the noun it explains.

1. My best friend Hetty Sullivan is traveling in Europe.
2. Have you met Mr. Rogers my English teacher?
3. Nantucket an old ship was on display at the Navy Yard.
4. That old tree a sturdy oak was struck by lightning.
5. Ben Franklin a man of many talents is remembered by all.

Create one sentence from each pair below. Use the information in the second sentence as an appositive to a word appearing in the first sentence.

Example: Kim can design clothes. She is my sister.
Kim, my sister, can design clothes.

6. Our new car uses very little gas. It is a Honda.

_____

7. We called Ms. Edwards. She is the art editor.

_____

8. Terry, this is Chico. He is my brother.

_____

9. Pat likes outdoor life. She is the girl in the yellow sweater.

_____

10. A young singer captivated the whole country. It was Michael Jackson.

_____

Write five sentences about friends or relatives. Use at least two appositives.

_____

_____

_____

_____

_____

 MP3457 Writing Well

Clauses and Phrases

Identify each underlined group of words as a phrase or clause. Write C on the line if the words are a clause. Write P if the words are a phrase.

*A **clause** contains a subject and a verb. A **phrase** is a group of words which acts as a single part of speech. It does not contain a subject or predicate.*

_____ 1. They made posters *for the class play*.

_____ 2. The house *with the green shutters* was sold.

_____ 3. The man *who lives next door* was taken to the hospital.

_____ 4. Sam's clothes were soaked *because he had no raincoat*.

_____ 5. The girl *in the brown coat* found your wallet.

_____ 6. My mother likes the outfit *that I bought yesterday*.

_____ 7. I shopped at the grocery store *by the new bank*.

_____ 8. We were curious about the cave *where they found the treasure*.

_____ 9. The book *which I read last week* was quite entertaining.

_____ 10. *I turned the key*, but the door wouldn't open.

_____ 11. *Although Simon loves school*, Jason hates it.

_____ 12. I waited for two hours, but *the bus never came*.

Write about something you and your friends have seen or done in winter. When you finish, underline some of the phrases and clauses you have used. Ask a friend to label phrases and clauses in your paper.

_____

_____

_____

_____

_____

_____

_____

_____

_____

4

Expanding Sentences

Expand these sentences by adding phrases or clauses on the blanks.

Examples: Bill ____ stood at the door.
Bill, dressed in his best suit, stood at the door.
We all drove into town ____.
We all drove into town that very evening.

Expanding sentences can make them more interesting.

1. The person _____ wanted a donation.

2. The boy _____ brought them happiness.

3. The family visited Spain _____ .

4. They rewarded the ones who _____ .

5. Jim fed the fish _____ .

6. The policeman stood _____ .

7. I put my coat and boots _____ .

8. Because _____ , we were very disappointed.

9. During the evening, _____ .

10. The swaying car raced _____ .

11. Dan did empty the trash _____ .

12. Sally hit the ball, and it _____ .

13. The gold and orange butterfly flew _____ .

14. If _____ , I am sure you will enjoy it.

Expand these sentences by adding prepositional phrases used as adjectives to modify or describe nouns or pronouns.

15. The little boy flew the kite. _____

_____

16. Everyone admired the cat. _____

_____

17. Parents attended the meeting. _____

_____

  MP3457 Writing Well

Personal Pronouns

An independent clause can stand alone as a sentence, but a dependent clause cannot.

> **Example:** He cried. (**independent**)
> because he spilled milk (**dependent**)

*An **independent clause** can stand alone as a sentence, but a **dependent clause** cannot.*

A complex sentence has one independent clause and one or more dependent clauses.

> **Example:** He cried because he had spilled milk.

Dependent clauses are often introduced by words such as the following:

after	before	that	where
although	if	when	wherever
because	since	whenever	while

Write two different complex sentences for each pair of sentences below. Use the word in parentheses to combine them.

> **Example:** (after) The party was over. We went to Martha's house.
> Variation 1: After the party was over, we went to Martha's house.
> Variation 2: We went to Martha's house after the party was over.

1. (because) The roads were closed. The snow fell heavily.

   _____

   _____

2. (before) The leader made a fire. The campers set up their tents.

   _____

   _____

3. (since) The weather turned warm. Pam plays tennis every day.

   _____

   _____

4. (if) Paul will come with us. We will go skating.

   _____

   _____

5. (when) Mary struck out. The game was over.

   _____

   _____

Compound Sentences

A compound sentence is made up of two or more independent clauses. Clauses may be joined by using a comma and a conjunction. *And, but, and or* are the most commonly used conjunctions. The conjunctions *yet, so, for,* and *nor* are good clues to compound sentences.

Example: The dog advanced a step, and it began snarling.

In the following, circle the conjunction and underline the simple subject in each part of the compound sentence with a single line. Underline the verb with a double line. The first one is complete as an example.

1. She sent her children to college, and each benefitted by the education.
2. Dr. Tibbs was visiting a patient, but his wife welcomed us.
3. Mr. Blewett was transferred to Oregon, so Ms. Ewell was sent here in his place.
4. I was worried about the old man, for he was desperately ill.
5. He was not interested in fame, nor did he care about wealth.
6. Sad stories appeal to some people, but humorous stories appeal to most of us.

Sometimes a sentence contains a compound subject or predicate, but the sentence is not compound.

Example: The dog advanced a step and began snarling.

Remember, a compound sentence is two complete sentences together. A sentence can be simple even when it has a compound subject, or predicate, or both. Read the sentences below. If a sentence is compound, add the necessary comma before the conjunction. Mark S in the blank at the end. If the sentence is not compound but has a compound part, decide which part is compounded. Write subject, predicate, *or* both *in the blank.*

7. You must overcome your bad temper or your temper will overcome you. _____
8. The first witness told his story so then I told mine. _____
9. The invitations were written and mailed. _____
10. No one was in sight but we heard the sound of footsteps. _____
11. David enjoyed reading books yet he disliked magazines. _____
12. The car salesman and his customer took a demonstration ride. _____

On another sheet of paper, write five sentences about school activities. Use compound sentences or compound structures.

A compound sentence *is made up of two or more independent clauses.*

7

Combining Sentences

Combine each pair of sentences. Rewrite them as one simple sentence with a compound subject or compound predicate.

1. Otters have two layers of fur. Beavers have two layers of fur.

   _____

2. A beaver uses its front teeth to cut down trees. It uses its teeth to peel off bark.

   _____

   _____

3. Otters swim rapidly. They dive for fish. _____

   _____

Make one sentence out of each set of sentences by combining adjectives and adverbs.

4. The cardinals were beautiful. They were red. They ate the seed daily.

   _____

5. Melting snow can cause floods. It can cause many floods. The floods can be disastrous. _____

   _____

6. Flood waters recede. They recede slowly. _____

   _____

Rewrite each pair of sentences by combining them into one sentence with an appositive.

7. Amy is my older sister. Amy goes to Pershing High School.

   _____

8. Ted is Tom's brother. Ted walks with us once in awhile.

   _____

Combine each pair of sentences into one sentence by using phrases or clauses.

9. Mary lost her paper. It was for English class. _____

   _____

10. Lisa watched a comedy. She felt like laughing. _____

    _____

11. He opened the gifts. Then we ate dessert. _____

    _____

8

Topic Sentences

A good straightforward paragraph begins with a topic sentence. It helps the reader know what to expect. If the writer has written a unified paragraph, the body of the writing will support and give details about the topic sentence. A good topic sentence states a central thought which will be developed in the paragraph. A useful topic sentence should not be too broad.

*A **topic sentence** helps the reader know what to expect.*

Topic: Pets I have owned. (This is too broad for one paragraph.)

Topic sentence: A furry raccoon lived at our house for one week. (The other sentences in the paragraph will explain how the raccoon came to your house and what happened.)

Indicate whether the following topics are too broad or satisfactory to be developed in one paragraph:

	Too Broad	Satisfactory
1. The major rivers of the world	_____	_____
2. Music through the years	_____	_____
3. My favorite dessert	_____	_____
4. Farming in colonial times	_____	_____
5. My bedroom	_____	_____

After each topic, write a good topic sentence for a paragraph.

6. A Useful Hobby

_____

7. A Summer Job

_____

8. A Family Outing

_____

9. The School Cafeteria

_____

10. A Surprise

_____

Choose one of the above topics and develop a paragraph. Begin with the topic sentence you wrote, and prepare a strong middle section to support your statement. The concluding sentence should refer back to the topic. Write your paragraph on the back of this paper or on a separate sheet of paper.

9

Writing Paragraphs

*Use what you know about a good paragraph to grade the paragraphs below. Read them and decide which one will receive **E** (excellent), **G** (good), **U** (unsatisfactory). Be ready to tell why you gave each the grade.*

Remember the rules of a good paragraph.

A Formal education is important and it usually starts with kindergarten. One learns to read and next there is arithmetic and science. High school has more extra-curricular activities for the students than the elementary school. Playing baseball and football is important to the boys, and girls dream of being a cheerleader. College helps a person prepare for a lifetime job.

Grade _____

B I will never forget my first day in school. I cried until noon when I was finally released to go home. The teacher tried to get me interested in games and songs. My mother had dressed me in a new dress and shoes. When I finally was home and had eaten my lunch, I asked why I had to wait until the next day to go back to school because it was fun.

Grade _____

C My education began at the age of five when I started kindergarten. My mother had dressed me in a new dress and shoes. After she left me at the door I cried until the teacher captured me with songs and games. Noon announced the end of my first step toward being an educated person.

Grade _____

Write a topic sentence for each topic below. Then choose one of these topics and write a complete paragraph on the back of this page.

1. Window Shopping: _____
2. TV Viewing: _____
3. Saturday Afternoon: _____
4. Having Your Picture Taken: _____
5. Good Health is Important: _____
6. Embarrassing Moments: _____
7. Homework: _____
8. The Sport I Like Best: _____
9. Chores: _____
10. Buying Gifts: _____

10

Using Exact Words

Try to use words that give a clear sense of your meaning. Use a dictionary or thesaurus to look for interesting words to replace "tired" or vague words.

Replace the italicized words in each sentence below. Write a new, improved sentence for each. Make interesting sentences by changing several words if necessary.

1. I left my *stuff* on the bus.

   _____

2. Mr. Barnes is a *nice* person.

   _____

3. We saw a lot of *things* on our trip.

   _____

4. The weather was *awful* yesterday.

   _____

5. We could see *a lot* from the top floor of the building.

   _____

6. Their new baseball player is *good.*

   _____

7. My friends thought your report was *good.*

   _____

8. The old man *went* down the sidewalk.

   _____

9. Everyone is *okay* now.

   _____

10. We thought the movie was *great.*

   _____

How many synonyms do you know for each of the following words? Write as many as you can. Then use a dictionary or thesaurus to add new ones to your lists.

look _____

mad _____

talk _____

walk _____

awful _____

Personification and Hyperbole

Writers often try to add interest by saying things in unusual ways. **Personification** gives human characteristics to things or ideas.

Example: The gypsy made his violin cry.

Hyperbole is an unreasonable exaggeration.

Example: "I've told you a million times to do your homework," shouted Mother.
(Mother has probably mentioned your homework many times; however, it is unlikely that the number is anywhere near a million.)

Are the following personification or hyperbole? Be ready to explain the reason for each choice.

Personification *gives human characteristics to things or ideas.* **Hyperbole** *is an unreasonable exaggeration.*

1. The desk groaned under his weight. _____

2. The wind sighed in the night. _____

3. I'm so tired that I could sleep forever. _____

4. The rain slapped me in the face. _____

5. I'll die if it rains for our picnic. _____

6. Tires screamed as the race began. _____

7. The vines clutched at my ankles. _____

8. He lost his head and hit the first person he saw. _____

9. Fear lived with us in that house. _____

10. She cried a gallon of tears. _____

Write five personifications and five hyperboles of your own.

_____

_____

_____

_____

_____

_____

_____

_____

_____

MP3457 Writing Well

Metaphors and Similes

Metaphors and similes are imaginative kinds of comparisons. They are known as figures of speech. Like personification, figures of speech can make writing more colorful.

The simile, which states a comparison between two unlike objects, makes use of the word like or as.

Example: He is as fat as a pig. He eats like a pig.

A metaphor, which merely suggests a comparison, gives an object the qualities of some other, unlike object.

Example: He was a lion in battle.

Tell whether the following are metaphors or similes. Underline the things that are being compared. The first one has been done for you.

Similes *state a comparison between two unlike objects.* **Metaphors** *merely suggest a comparison.*

1. The sick child was a grouchy little bear.   _____*metaphor*_____

2. She is as happy as a lark.   _____

3. The tiny baby looks like an angel.   _____

4. Marvin is a cool cat.   _____

5. You're a fox for thinking of that idea.   _____

6. The baseball whizzed by like a bullet.   _____

7. The people looked like ants far below us.   _____

8. Our house was as quiet as a tomb.   _____

9. The coffee is like ink.   _____

10. She is a busy bee working in the garden.   _____

11. This street is a bottleneck.   _____

Write five similes and five metaphors of your own. You can find some in the newspaper and comic strips. Use the back of this paper if necessary.

_____

_____

_____

_____

_____

MP3457 Writing Well

Descriptive Paragraph

Good descriptive writing creates pictures in the reader's mind. Such writing often appeals to the senses: sight, smell, touch, taste, and hearing.

Sharpen your senses. Choose someone or something to observe closely and record your observations below. Try to use exact words and paint a vivid picture. You may use phrases instead of complete sentences.

Good descriptive writing creates pictures in the reader's mind.

Object or Person Observed

_____

_____

_____

_____

_____

_____

_____

Now work your observations into a descriptive paragraph. How will you begin? Descriptive paragraphs do not always have topic sentences. Whether or not you use a topic sentence for your paragraph, do use a lively opener to capture the interest of your reader. Include at least one metaphor or simile.

_____

_____

_____

_____

_____

_____

_____

_____

Share your paper with another person. Ask your editor to underline those parts of your paragraph that give a clear picture. Ask the reader to circle anything that is vague or unclear.

14

Words Create Moods

An author uses certain words and phrases to create an overall feeling or mood.

Place an (X) before those phrases that give you a feeling of happiness.

___ youngsters splashing in a lake

___ chirping birds and chattering squirrels

___ blue skies and brilliant sunlight

___ a warm fire on a cold evening

___ spectators cheering for their winning team

___ ruined, dried up crops

___ downcast eyes

___ loud laughter

___ long wails of despair

___ dark, threatening clouds

Moods *are created by the careful selection of words.*

On the back of this paper write a paragraph using the phrases you have marked as giving a feeling of happiness. Weave them into a short story that creates a happy mood.

Place an (X) before those phrases that give a feeling of uneasiness or anxiety about something unpleasant that might happen.

___ low rumble of thunder

___ bending, clutching trees

___ yellow sunflowers

___ howling in the distance

___ trees moaning in the wind

___ sleeping dog at your feet

___ swaying shadows

___ trembling hands

___ cheering crowd

___ a muddy river rushing out of its banks

Write another short paragraph using the uncomfortable phrases you have marked above. When you finish your paragraph, have a classmate read it to see if you did create a mood of uneasiness. _____

_____

_____

_____

On a separate sheet of paper write an entire story in which you begin with the feeling of happiness or calmness and then change to uneasiness or panic. Before the story ends, try to come back to a calm mood.

In a comic strip, the mood is often created with details in the pictures. Find examples to show how the artist has set the mood. It is more difficult to create mood with words alone. Find examples in newspaper stories. Circle and share some mood phrases.

What Can I Write?

A good story teller helps readers sense the moods of his or her characters. The words below describe different moods or the spirit in which a person may act or speak.

A well written story should reflect the moods of its characters.

distressed	disgusted	sympathetic	determined
discontented	envious	lonely	triumphant
angry	sad	vexed	amazed
spiteful	bewildered	amused	mischievous
guilty	shy	lazy	joyful

Read the direct quotations below. Decide which of the words above best describes the mood of the person speaking. You may use more than one of the words for each blank. Use a dictionary to help you understand the shades of meaning for some of the words.

1. "Michele's new dress is so lovely! I wish I had one for the party," sighed Lilli.

   Lilli is _____.

2. "I should have called Joe and invited him to the same party, but I forgot," said Sam.

   Sam is _____.

3. "The grass is so high, and there is so much to mow that by the time I finish, I'll have to start over," moaned Larry.

   Larry is _____.

4. "I know how you feel. My dog was sick once, and we were afraid she would never get well," soothed Molly.

   Molly is _____.

5. "The answer to this problem just won't come to me. I guess I'll never understand arithmetic," gasped Jack.

   Jack is _____.

7. "Let's put a rubber spider on Ken's chair. I like playing jokes," whispered Jill.

   Jill is _____.

Use the back of this paper. Create several situations in which the mood of the speaker is revealed by what is said. See if your classmates can discover your characters' moods.

Direct Quotation

A direct quotation tells us the exact words spoken by someone. These words are enclosed within quotation marks (""). They may appear at the beginning, middle, or end of a sentence. They may even be split. In the examples, notice the use of the comma, capital letters, and other punctuation marks.

Examples:
1. "We can't come to the party," replied Jane.
2. Father asked, "Didn't anyone empty the trash?"
3. "I thought," murmured Jean, "you were right behind me."

Dialogue is conversation between two or more persons. It is nothing but conversation expressed in quotations. The writer uses the rules which apply to punctuating a direct quotation. Authors must use words other than *said* or *asked* to help the readers feel the mood or spirit in which a dialogue is spoken. Here are different ways of saying *said*:

declared	gasped	murmured	boasted	answered
whispered	giggled	admitted	shouted	begged
croaked	added	demanded	stated	shrieked
remarked	exclaimed	reported	stammered	suggested
groaned	commented	advised	questioned	inquired

Punctuate the following dialogues. Use capitals wherever necessary. Choose a word from the list above that helps tell how the dialogue is spoken. Try to use each word only once. Notice that a new paragraph must be started each time the speaker changes.

1. Sandy, you are too little to use my camera put it down _____ Gene
   But I just wanted to see how it worked _____ Sandy
   All right I'll show you how it works _____ Gene but then go away so I can work

2. Mary _____ it is a lovely day for skating on Turner's Pond
   Yes Mary and there are some of our friends _____ Jo over by the fire
   Suddenly Mary _____ turn back the ice is breaking

3. My throat is so sore _____ Heather I don't know how I will be able to sing my solo
   Maybe they could cancel your part Lee _____

4. Oh no my grandmother has come from Albany to hear me sing _____ Heather and she would be so disappointed

Using some of the other ways to say said, *write two simple dialogues of your own. Think of some words other than those suggested above.*

17

A **direct quotation** *tells us the exact words spoken by someone.*

Creating Characters

Good writers are able to make characters seem real. They use various techniques to picture their characters, such as:

1. Straightforward description of physical characteristics
2. Telling about a character's actions, thoughts, or speech
3. Giving the reactions of other characters *to* the character

There are various techniques to make characters seem real.

Reveal a character's feelings. Think of a person you know well. Describe four feelings such as sadness, anger, loneliness, joy, worry, love, concern, etc. you have seen your friend have. Write about an action to show each feeling.

_____

_____

_____

_____

_____

_____

Describe a character's traits such as friendly, helpful, courageous, active, forgetful, cautious, etc. Think of a person you know well. Write four of his or her traits.

_____

_____

_____

_____

_____

Create a character. Write a description of your character that includes the following: physical characteristics, traits, feelings. Include an action or example to illustrate traits and feelings.

_____

_____

_____

_____

_____

_____

Creating Settings

A story takes place in a specific location and at a certain time. The place and time make the setting. It is often an important element of a story.

Practice creating settings. You will need to activate your imagination, your senses, and your vocabulary.

Describe a place where you had an enjoyable time. Include at least four sights and sounds you remember. _____

_____

_____

_____

The place and time in which a story takes place is its setting.

Describe a place where you were uncomfortable (bored, frightened, uneasy). Include at least four sights and sounds you remember. _____

_____

_____

_____

_____

_____

_____

Create an imaginary setting. It might be a world or town you have invented. Use at least five details to describe it. _____

_____

_____

_____

_____

_____

_____

_____

_____

_____

_____

_____

19

Creating a Plot

The events of a story make up its **plot**.

Practice creating plots. Use other paper to continue your stories.

The events of a story make up its **plot**.

1. Imagine a time machine that takes you into the future. Write five details about life in this future time. _____
   _____
   _____

Many stories have problems that need to be solved. The plots center around attempts to solve the problems.

2. Think of a problem you have actually had at some time. List three different ways this problem might be solved (or at least how someone might attempt to solve it). _____
   _____
   _____
   _____

3. Think of a problem you have heard or read about. You might select a problem situation from the newspaper. List two or three attempts to solve it. Then tell how it was finally solved.

   Problem: _____
   _____

   Attempts to solve the problem: _____
   _____
   _____

   Solution: _____
   _____

4. Sometimes adventures form the plot of a story. Think of an adventure you would like to have. Describe it as though it really happened.
   _____
   _____
   _____

5. Select one of your plot ideas. Add character and setting details and write a story on another sheet of paper.

20

Writing a First Person Narrative

A **narrative** tells a story or event. The narrator is the person telling the story. A narrator may take part in the story or may be an outside observer. When the narrator tells the story as a participating member and uses pronouns such as **I**, **we**, **us**, the narrative is said to be in the **first person**.

Imagine that you are a character in a well-known fairy tale, book, or movie. Tell the story, or one of the events in the story, in the first person (from your character's point of view). Include some of the character's thoughts and feelings.

_____

_____

_____

_____

_____

_____

_____

_____

_____

_____

_____

_____

_____

_____

_____

_____

_____

_____

_____

_____

_____

_____

_____

Trade papers with someone. Offer compliments and suggestions for improvements to each other. Revise your composition if necessary.

21

Five Ws In Reporting

The five Ws in writing: Who, What, When, Where, and How or Why.

The first paragraph in a news story is called a lead. In one or two sentences, the lead usually answers most of the following questions:

1. **Who** (or what) is involved?
2. **What** happened?
3. **When** did it happen?
4. **Where** did it happen?
5. **How** or **Why** did it happen?

Further descriptions and details are then included in later paragraphs.

Local Hero Honored

Jay Jacks received a plaque at a dinner Saturday honoring him for saving two small children from drowning.

On his way home from school Tuesday, Jay heard muffled cries for help coming from Skater's Pond. He ran to the pond and rescued Sandy and Bill Boas from the icy water into which they had fallen.

Who?_____ What?_____

When?_____ Where? _____

Why or How?_____

Ho Hums to Perform

The newest music group, the Ho Hums, will give a benefit performance on February 14, 2002, at Hope Auditorium. All proceeds will go to the Organ Fund for research.

Who? _____ What?_____

When?_____ Where? _____

Why or How?_____

Storm Cripples Northern City

A severe blizzard blanketed the city of Faraway, Maine, last night with a 24-inch snowfall, accompanied by 60 mph winds.

As Phillip Moore, the mayor, declared the town a disaster area, the weary residents began to dig out from under the snow drifts, some of which reached a depth of 8 feet.

Who?_____ What?_____

When?_____ Where? _____

Why or How?_____

Feature stories can be very interesting. Features tell about impressive people or unusual events. A feature story may be an interview with a famous person visiting your town. Find a feature story and bring it to class for everyone to enjoy.

News Stories With the Five Ws

Write a news story. Use the following facts and pretend you are a cub reporter. Add a good headline.

Who? Geraldine Grant   **What?** Elected class president
When? Sunday Afternoon   **Where?** Deerfoot University
                                                Why or **How?** Largest number of votes

The five Ws in writing: Who, What, When, Where, and How or Why.

_____

_____

_____

_____

_____

_____

_____

_____

_____

Write your very own news story. Be sure it contains the 5Ws and some details. Prepare a good headline for your story.

_____

_____

_____

_____

_____

_____

_____

_____

_____

_____

_____

_____

_____

23

A Persuasive Paragraph

Writers sometimes want others to agree with their opinions. They try to convince, or persuade, the reader with good reasons and strong arguments. One way to write a persuasive paragraph is to build toward a climax. Try writing a persuasive paragraph by following these suggestions.

*A **persuasive paragraph** tries to convince, or persuade, the reader.*

1. *Decide on a topic. It might be about homework, watching television, a certain school or family rule, pollution, some current event or controversy in the news. Plan to write your paragraph as an advertisement, a book review, or a letter to the editor of a newspaper or magazine.*

2. *Compose a topic sentence that states your major argument. State what you are trying to convince your reader to do, think, or believe.*

3. *List reasons and facts that will help persuade your reader to agree with you.*

4. *Number your arguments 1,2,3, and so on. Use 1 as the strongest argument.*

5. *Write the paragraph following this order:*
   - Topic sentence
   - Arguments in sequence beginning with the weakest and stating the strongest one last
   - A summary statement

_____

_____

_____

_____

_____

_____

_____

_____

_____

_____

_____

_____

_____

_____

MP3457 Writing Well

Explanatory Paragraph

Write a paragraph that gives an explanation. Follow these steps:

1. *Decide on the topic to be explained. Choose a topic that does not have too many steps.*

2. *List the steps.*

3. *Put the steps in correct order.*

4. *Choose a few signal words (such as first, then, finally, next) to help reinforce the order.*

5. *Compose a topic sentence that hints at the topic.*
   Suggestions for topic sentences:

   ● If you want to _____, you should follow these few steps.
   ● _____ is easy if you know the secret.
   ● Making a _____ is rewarding and fun.
   ● There are steps that you should follow in _____.

*An **explanatory paragraph** is meant to explain a topic.*

You may want to begin with an introductory sentence that catches the reader's attention. The introductory sentence would then come before the topic sentence.

> **Example:** Have you ever heard of Barbarian's Delight? My sisters and I used to make them on snowy days. They are delicious. First, you . . .

6. *Complete your paragraph by adding necessary details.*

7. *You may want to include a summing-up at the end.*

Use the blanks below to plan your explanatory paragraph.

Topic: _____

_____

Introductory sentence (optional): _____

_____

Topic sentence (See suggestions above): _____

_____

Details: _____

_____

_____

Now write your paragraph neatly on another paper.

25

A Friendly Letter

Make corrections in the two letters and the envelope below. The circles indicate places where corrections or additions are needed.

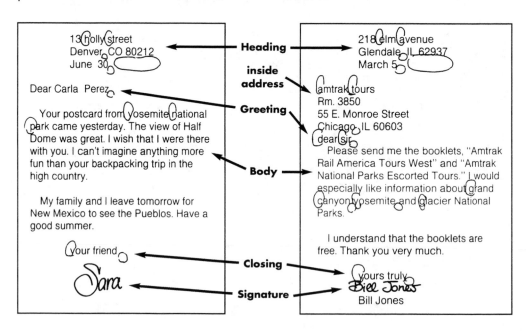

Write a friendly letter telling about a trip you've taken, answering an invitation, thanking someone for a gift, or describing a sports event at school.

Write a business letter requesting information, ordering something, explaining why you are returning a product you ordered, or asking permission for your class to visit a local business or factory.

MP3457 Writing Well

Proofreading Symbols

Proofreading what is written before it is put into final form is very important. There are certain symbols used by professional proofreaders that should be familiar to everyone. Some of the most frequently used are:

¶ Start a new paragraph.   I have a dog Insert at this point.

≡ Capitalize the letter.   dont Insert the punctuation indicated.

used are Reverse the position of the words or letter; transpose.   go to Leave a space.

ℓ.c. ⫽ Lower case (no capital) Margin note: l.c.   sp. (mak) Circle what is misspelled. Margin note: SP

There are certain symbols used by professional proofreaders that should be familiar to everyone.

You Are the Proofreader

Use the correct proofreading symbols to mark the corrections needed to make this composition correct.

What Is Beautiful

What dose beautiful mean. Dose it mean Graceful Powerful Exciting amazing Mysterious simple Groovy Dose it mean someone you hope to meet.

To a studant, it is an "A". To a teem, it is a vistory. Toa teacher, it a vacation. To a blind man, it is sight. To a deef man, it is sound. Is ther anyone who has never siad beautiful. I will tellyou what is baeutiful to me, and You tell what is beautiful to you. Let me start with faces. To me faces are beautiful, young are old. Young faces show wander at each newthing. Old faces reflect wisdom ineach wrinkle. faces are the windows of our soles, instruments love andmurals ofour lives

Action is beautiful — a mud-spatered quaterback huging the ball while zig-zags toward a touchdow, a sleak car whizzing down the highway. Swimmrs gracefully slicing and silently gliding through crystal water Strolling among fallen autum leafs — action is beautiful! Life is beautiful — a flowreing plant a puppy scarlet birds drooling babies, youg people in love. These are all beautufl.

Beautiful meens even more then these things. Not all things are Beautiful, but beauty surrounds each one of us and is waiting to be caught by the eye of the beholder.

On a separate sheet of paper write a composition describing what beautiful means to you.

27

Comma and Quotation Checkup

Prove that you know where and when to use commas, quotation marks, and other punctuation marks which help your reader understand your purpose.

Insert the proper punctuation where needed, and capitalize wherever necessary.

*Do you know when and where to use a **comma**?*

1. Put the saw hammer screwdriver and wrench in the tool box
2. May would you like to come skating with us
3. He moved to Boston massachusetts on December 20 1980
4. It was Perry who said we have met the enemy and they are ours
5. Yes Dale went to the store for a loaf of bread
6. The principal announced there is a storm coming and we will dismiss early
7. Robert Fulton the inventor of the steamboat was a misunderstood man
8. Boys stop looking out of the window while I am teaching commanded Ms. Green
9. You can say what you want but we don't have to agree
10. The fluffy clouds are like cotton puffs Jennifer said wistfully
11. Necessary fishing equipment includes a pole line hook sinker and bait
12. Geraniums good house plants come in many colors
13. It was only a minor accident yet traffic was blocked for an hour
14. This is not the correct answer Robert
15. It is better advised the clerk to send the package by express

Write a sentence to use each of the following:

- commas in a list (series)
- commas in an appositive
- a direct quotation
- a comma in a date
- a comma to set off the name of a person being addressed

_____

_____

_____

_____

_____

_____

_____

_____

_____

28